TANKERS
GIANTS OF THE SEA

TANKERS
GIANTS OF THE SEA

By Charles Coombs
illustrated with photographs

William Morrow and Company
New York 1979

Library of Congress Cataloging in Publication Data

Coombs, Charles Ira, 1914-
  Tankers, giants of the sea.

  Includes index.
  Summary: Discusses the use of tankers as oil-carrying vehicles, their construction, and life aboard them.
  1. Tankers—Juvenile literature. [1. Tankers. 2. Ships. 3. Petroleum industry and trade] I. Title.
VM455.C64   387.2′45   79-9376
ISBN 0-688-22205-6
ISBN 0-688-32205-0 lib. bdg.

Printed in the United States of America.
1 2 3 4 5 6 7 8 9 10

J
387.2
C

Permission is gratefully acknowledged:

Alyeska Pipeline Service, 111,114; American Petroleum Institute, 13,18,35, 108,116; Atlantic Richfield Company, 21,53,59,61 bottom, 66,99; Author, 56,61 top, 63,64,90,91,92,94,101,102,103,106; Bethlehem Steel Corporation, 15,41,42,44,46,49,85; Chevron, 58; Continental Oil Company, 12,104; General Dynamics Corporation, 34; Gulf Oil Corporation, 29,31,32; Jacksonville Shipyards, Inc., 45; Loop, Inc., 117,118; Mobil Oil Corporation, 87,120,122; United States Coast Guard, 71,76,78,80,82.

CONTENTS

FOREWORD

Whenever possible, I try to include some adventure when researching a book. I have explored the blockhouses and launch pads of Cape Canaveral, fought off frostbite on Alaska's North Slope, been on hand during exploration of the ocean deeps. I have tooled around in all sorts of wheeled vehicles, and either actively or vicariously enjoyed the excitement of many sports.

But topping all these experiences was a recent round-trip winter voyage aboard the Atlantic Richfield Company's 120,000-dwt crude-oil tanker, the SS *Arco Fairbanks,* up the Pacific Coast to Valdez, Alaska. In the midst of a serious energy crisis, it seemed important to me to try and find out what oil tankers are like, what they do, and why they are needed.

After reading all I could about these behemoths of the sea, I boarded the empty *Fairbanks* in Long Beach, California. As we sailed north, I had the run of the vessel, from bilge to bridge. Keeping out of the way of officers and deckhands, I was able to observe closely everything that took place aboard the tanker.

I peered over shoulders, peeked through hatches, and asked endless questions. The answers I received were prompt, candid, and, I have every reason to believe, honest. Tankering is good, if sometimes lonely, work. Seamen know that their ships will be around for as long as the world depends on crude oil for energy and petroleum products. Few nations are energy-independent; therefore, oil must be sent by sea to those countries that have purchased it.

I had heard and read frightening stories concerning careless shipping practices, dumping of oil ballast at sea, and other environmental horrors. So I kept my eyes open for anything untoward. However, I found that concern about the environment reaches well out to sea.

To say that I was impressed with the operation

8

of the *Arco Fairbanks* is to put it mildly. The ship was immaculate, and despite sudden changes in the delivery schedule, and what I considered a horrendous storm, which struck while we were northbound in the Gulf of Alaska, the vessel completed its mission on time and without mishap. "What storm?" the captain asked the next morning, puzzled by my dramatized version of the sleepless, sea-tossed night.

Of course, I cannot speak for all ships. Yet, there are local, Federal, and international laws regulating tanker operations, and agencies to enforce them. So I returned home greatly encouraged by what I had seen and heard.

To all the seafarers who man the *Fairbanks,* and particularly to Captain Robert Lawlor, my most sincere thanks for a fantastic voyage.

Charles "Chick" Coombs
Westlake Village, California, 1979

1
THE BIG SHIPS

There are more tankers in the world than ships of any other kind. They vary greatly in size. Some are small short-haul vessels that carry a few hundred tons of crude oil or petroleum products. Others are great steel giants that haul half a million or more tons of liquid cargo in their cavernous tanks. These tankers are the biggest moving objects ever built by man.

Waterborne oil carriers sail all the oceans. They shuttle back and forth across lakes and navigate the major inland waterways of most countries. On an average day, some seventy million tons of oil and petroleum products are transported over water.

The primary purpose of these tankers is to carry

11

Crude-oil tankers are the largest manmade moving objects in the world.

the oil from where it is brought out of the earth to where it will be refined and converted into useful products.

Most large oil fields are located in remote areas of the world, far from population centers and commercial markets. Essential to the operation of automobiles, trucks, boats, and buses, oil also fuels the machines of industry. It is needed to heat homes and factories, to generate electricity, to provide organic chemicals for medicines, and to

12

manufacture an infinite variety of products required in modern life.

This need for petroleum products—gasoline, jet fuel, diesel oil, paraffin, fuel oil, and petrochemicals—has made oil the world's biggest and most important item of trade. No nation can survive without it, so despite the political, environmental, and financial problems involved, there must be means to distribute it.

Pipelines, railroad tank cars, and tanker trucks

Tankers line up in the Port of Dammam, Saudi Arabia.

carry petroleum overland quite efficiently. But three quarters of the Earth's surface is covered with water. In order to move crude oil and the products made from it over the ocean, lakes, rivers, and canals of the world, an enormous fleet of specialized tankers has come into being. The massive liquid cargoes they carry make up more than a third of the total tonnage transported by merchant ships of all sizes and kinds. Oil tankers, indeed, dominate the world's waterways.

Figures are not easily come by, for the number of tankers varies almost daily. A fair estimate is that there are about 4,000 tankships with capacities of over 10,000 deadweight tons in operation. In addition, there are several thousand small, short-haul, shallow-draft river tankers and canal barges, which have a much lower deadweight-ton capacity. (A deadweight ton (dwt) is the unit by which a tanker's cargo, fuel, and stores are normally measured. Deadweight-ton measurements are made in 2,240-pound long tons rather than in the more familiar 2,000-pound short tons. Deadweight ratings do not include the weight of the ship itself, which is known as displacement.)

14

A comparatively small 37,000-dwt tanker
carries petrochemical products.

Of the 4,000 seagoing tankers, roughly eight
hundred can be classified as superships or supertankers. They are by far the largest objects afloat,
but the classification of super has become so com-
monplace that few tankermen use it anymore.
Following World War II, any tanker with more

than a 25,000-dwt capacity was considered a supertanker. In that era of small merchant ships, people marveled at their size. As tankers continued to grow larger, the supertanker label was reserved for seaborne oil tankers that could haul in excess of 50,000 dwt's. Soon that figure escalated to 100,000 dwt's, which are big ships even by today's standards. However, during the 1960s and 1970s, even the 100,000-tonners gave way to still bigger ships, and the label of supertankers became outmoded again.

So the tankermen developed more accurate titles to give the enormous vessels coming out of shipyards. They began calling the tankships having between 160,000- and 300,000-dwt capacity Very Large Crude Carriers (VLCCs). Most of the bigger ships added to the tanker fleet during the 1970s fell into that class. Those ships that ranged from 300,000 dwt to over half a million tons—and quite a few such tankers began appearing—were called Ultra Large Crude Carriers (ULCCs). Thus, the new labels—very large or ultra large—came into being. Although the nonseafaring public and the news media are still inclined to group all the big ships under the convenient name of super-tanker, VLCC and ULCC are more accurate definitions.

There are, of course, several reasons why the size of oil tankers kept growing. Too many small tankers were taking too long to meet the world's ever-increasing petroleum needs.

Many of the small tankers were getting old, corroded, and leaky. Improperly fitted out with overused powerplants and lacking updated controls and navigational instruments, many were hazards to shipping. They were candidates for the scrap pile.

Furthermore, on a cost-per-ton basis, one big tanker is cheaper to build than several small ones. This so-called economy of scale works in several ways. *Adding* to a tanker's dimensions *multiplies* its capacity. For instance, a VLCC tanker that carries 200,000 dwt's might be only twice as long and two times as wide as a small 20,000-dwt vessel. Yet it carries ten times as much oil.

The economy of scale also applies to the crew. Whatever its size, the number of officers and seamen needed to operate a ship remains relatively

e size of tankers has grown over the years.

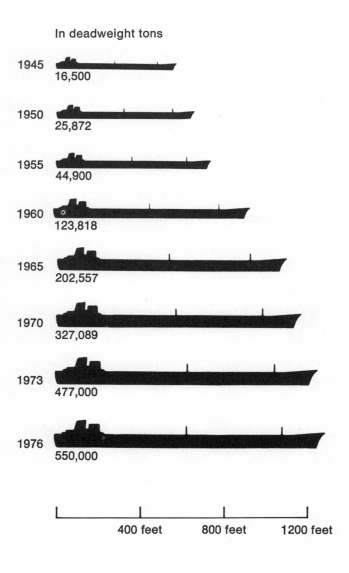

In deadweight tons

1945 16,500

1950 25,872

1955 44,900

1960 123,818

1965 202,557

1970 327,089

1973 477,000

1976 550,000

| | 400 feet | 800 feet | 1200 feet |

the same. Because big modern tankers are virtually automated, often fewer crew members are
needed aboard a VLCC than on much smaller
tankers. From deep down in the engine room to
high on the captain's bridge, operating the ship
is a matter of reading dials, pushing buttons,
watching radarscopes, and moving levers only
when sophisticated instruments say they should
be moved.

Another economic benefit from large tankers is
the comparative reduction in the amount of power
needed to propel it and the saving in fuel. In proportion to its size, the big ship's hull is hydro-
dynamically more efficient than a small hull. A
200,000-dwt VLCC moves through the water with
much less friction or resistance than would be
generated by four 50,000-dwt tankers. As a result,
the bigger ship can operate on less than half the
horsepower needed to turn the propellers of the
four smaller ones.

Because of all these factors, oil that is transported in one large tanker instead of several small
ones can be two or three cents a gallon cheaper.
Considering that a VLCC can carry nearly 100

million gallons of crude, the savings can amount to millions of dollars in a single voyage.

Of course, a big vessel can cause a big spill. Yet, shipowners and operators argue that there is far less congestion with fewer tankers and far less risk of accidents. Fewer crews at sea should mean fewer chances of human error, and again, fewer accidents. An experienced skipper and a well-trained crew can navigate and maneuver a large automated vessel almost as easily as a small one. Aside from the massive consequences of a serious accident, most arguments strongly favor the use of large vessels in global transportation.

Some tankers are owned outright or carry long-term charters by the petroleum company whose products they transport. The officers and crew of such tankers usually are employees of the company's marine department. Many of these ships are American-built and carry United States registry. They are known as American-flag tankers and are used primarily to distribute oil and petroleum products between ports of call along the United States coastline. Typical of American-flag ships

The 120,000-dwt *Arco Fairbanks* is designed for
the shallow-water ports of the United States.

are the tankers that shuttle in and out of the port
of Valdez, Alaska.

By law, American-flag ships are operated by
American crews, and repairs and maintenance are
done in American shipyards. Such regulations,
plus the relatively high wages paid to American
officers and seamen, make running an American-
flag vessel more expensive than a tanker sailing
under foreign registry, or a so-called flag of con-
venience.

There are plenty of big tankers available for hire. So many have been built in fact, that at this writing there is a glut of them. Because there is not enough petroleum trade to keep them all busy, some lie inactive in remote harbors. Others serve as floating storage tanks anchored offshore.

A majority of oil tankers fly foreign flags. Most of these ships are privately owned and are available for hire by oil companies. Ships from England, Japan, Italy, France, Greece, and Scandinavia are common in tanker sea-lanes. However, by far the largest single fleet of tankers in the world carries the flag of Liberia. Strangely, this small West African nation does not produce oil, build tankers, or provide crews. It is not in the oil-transportation business nor does it own ships.

Liberia, and other countries such as Panama and Malaysia, simply allow shipowners to register vessels with them and operate under their flag. They charge a fee for the privilege, but the fee is nominal in comparison to what most other nations charge, and shipowners are willing to pay it.

Lower insurance and crew costs and fewer maintenance restrictions make operating a tanker under a foreign flag economically desirable. For this reason, big United States oil-transporting companies tend to use American-flag tankers in domestic waters and foreign-flag ships for most of their worldwide trade.

There is some doubt whether foreign-flag ships are as efficiently and safely operated or as well maintained as the more rigidly regulated American ships. However, regardless of the flag a tanker carries, it must abide by local laws of the countries it serves, as well as international agreements and established rules of the sea.

A company may take a long-term charter on a tanker rather than buy it outright. It provides the crew and operates the ship for a given period of time, perhaps as long as the tanker remains seaworthy. By chartering instead of owning, the company escapes involvement in complicated financing. A tanker that costs eighty million dollars to build goes through many levels of financing before it is finally paid off.

The advantage of a long-term charter over a short-term or spot charter is that the company is sure to have the tanker at its disposal whenever it is needed. A spot charterer may get caught with a big order or a rush call for oil and no available ship to haul it.

Whether owned, chartered, leased, or rented, an oil tanker must be kept busy. It is too expensive to be left idle. Like an airliner or an interstate truck, it must be kept on the move day and night, stopping only to load or unload its cargo. Loan payments, charter fees, crew wages, and operating costs continue whether or not the ship is at work.

Yet no matter how hard the captain of a tanker tries to maintain a regular schedule, he cannot always do so. Heading into a storm may drastically reduce a ship's normal speed. A captain may slow down and alter course so the ship will take the violent waves bow on and prevent extensive strain or damage to the hull. Such action may even prevent the ship from breaking up and sinking. But these delays cannot always be made up, and schedules sometimes slip.

Normally, an oil tanker is a one-purpose vessel. It loads up with oil, sails many thousands of miles to discharge its cargo, then goes back for more. On its return, it sails empty or in ballast. There is no profit in sailing an empty ship, so some vessels are being constructed or adapted to carry other kinds of cargo. Such ships are known as combination vessels. In one direction, they transport oil or petroleum products. Then, on the return trip, they haul a load of coal or ore. If the tanks have been properly cleaned, they might even carry a load of corn, wheat, or some other bulky item. These combination vessels are designated as OBO's—oil/bulk/ore carriers.

There are complications, however, in the very concept of OBO's. Most of the places where a tanker goes for oil are probably not in need of a shipload of corn. A handy iron mine is not often available near the port where oil is discharged. Yet a ship can be reasonably flexible: it can afford to alter its course somewhat if a return load makes it profitable to do so.

Tankers have been around for a century or so. They have helped make history and will continue to do so as long as fossil fuels remain the primary source of energy. The big ships are here to stay.

2
EARLY OIL TRANSPORT

Delivering oil by ship has been going on as long as civilization itself. More than five thousand years ago, Greeks, Romans, and Phoenicians shipped oil throughout the Mediterranean coastal areas. Olive oil rather than petroleum, it was carried in jars, wooden vats, or baked clay amphoras instead of in the vessel itself. This olive oil was used to light lamps, for cooking, on the skin, in perfume, and was thought to have high medicinal value.

As far back as the seventh century B.C., these same Mediterranean people discovered that they could burn the black liquid they sometimes found seeping up from underground. It was good for lubricating wheel axles, too, and it kept down the dust effectively when sprinkled on chariot roads. This so-called earth oil soon became an item of trade and was transported in a variety of containers loaded aboard ships.

Not until the middle of the eighteenth century, however, did this black oil begin to come into its own. New machines were replacing old-fashioned hand tools. The machines required fuel to operate and lubricants to reduce the friction of moving parts. Oil answered both of these needs, and ever-increasing amounts were shipped in large tin cases or barrels. It was in short supply, though, and whale oil and coal remained popular.

Then, in 1859, in Titusville, Pennsylvania, the first successful oil strike in the United States occurred. A new industry was born. The petroleum age was under way. Overnight there was an urgent need for ships to transport the crude oil to places where it could be refined and processed and then to carry the petroleum products to markets around the world.

Wooden barges were built to ferry containers of oil up rivers and across lakes. Many sailing ships that normally hauled bulk cargo were fitted out to carry large tanks or barrels of oil. The first such ship in the United States, a converted brig named the *Elizabeth Watts*, sailed for London with a full cargo of oil in 1861. Before the end of the Civil War, the United States was exporting approximately thirty-two million gallons of oil a year. Pumps were installed to discharge the oil from the ship's tanks at the ports of call. Extra barrels of crude oil, or of refined products such as kerosene, often would be racked on the deck to fill out the cargo.

The real forerunner of modern tankers was built in England in 1886 for a German-American oil company. The ship was called the *Glückauf* ("good luck" in German). Although basically a steamship, the *Glückauf* also carried sails to assist the engine-driven propeller when needed. The vessel's most important feature, however, was that the iron hull served as the oil tank. There was no longer any need for barrels, casks, or other containers. The ship *was* the tank.

In order to carry a maximum amount of oil—nearly a million gallons—the bulky engine normally located near the middle of the ship was

At turn of the century oil was carried in barrels
or tanks aboard general cargo ships.

placed far aft. The vessel's bridge structure and
officers' quarters remained amidships as was typical of most ships of the day, but the smokestack
and crew's quarters were shifted toward the stern.
A raised forecastle helped protect the bow against
battering waves and provided space for paint,
rope, spare parts, and other ship's stores.

For the sake of the ship's stability under way, the large cargo space amidships was divided by bulkheads into a number of smaller tanks. This design eliminated dangerous sloshing that might overturn the ship. It also enabled the cargo officer to distribute the load so as to insure smooth, safe sailing. In case of an accident, the spill would be limited to a single small tank rather than an entire hull.

This basic oil-tanker design was used for nearly seventy years. There were not enough such sea-going tankers, however, to take care of wartime needs. During World War I, for example, the Allies modified every possible ship to carry oil to the fighting forces. Dry-cargo holds often were adapted to hold liquids. Some ships even resorted to hauling oil in their ballast tanks.

As liquid cargoes are extremely heavy, loads had to be kept small to prevent the ship from snapping its rivets in a heavy sea or breaking up and sinking. When riveting began to give way to welding and the more durable steel started to replace iron in hull construction, tankships became immensely stronger and leakproof.

A three-island oil tanker

During World War II a large fleet of American tankers known as T-2's convoyed critically needed petroleum products through the German-U-boat-filled waters. They figured prominently in the eventual victory. Following the war, these 16,-500-dwt ships, large for their time, continued to dominate the tanker lanes. Often a standard T-2 was jumboized by splitting the vessel in half and adding an extra section of hull in the middle. In this way the tanker's capacity was doubled. Today a few T-2's are still sailing even after forty years of service.

Like the *Glückauf*, the T-2's were three-island ships, having a raised forecastle, navigation bridge and officers' quarters amidships, and engine room and crew quarters far astern.

In the mid-1950s, a major change took place in tanker design. The midshiphouse structure that interrupted the clean sweep of the weather deck was eliminated entirely. Everything that did not have to do with oil storage was moved toward the stern with the engines. The single aft superstructure was enlarged to include the officers' accommodations, the galley and wardrooms, the radio shack, and the captain's cabin. The navigation bridge and chartroom were placed at the topmost level. The entire forward hull was now tank space.

Larger tankers still had a midshiphouse,
although the machinery was moved to the stern.

Stretching in front of the aft superstructure was open deck space, broken only by the winches, davits, hawser bitts, and fairleads needed to handle the many ropes and cables used during docking operations. Powerful windlasses for hoisting the heavy anchors were located on the foredeck. Kingposts were added amidships to support loading booms needed for handling heavy hoses, moving the gangway ladder, or doing other lifting chores. Around and over all was a spaghettilike array of pipes, tubing, valves, and gauges that moved the oil cargo.

In more recent years, a new class of tankers has emerged. Some look similar to an oil tanker; others seem to be carrying monstrous metal balloons in their hulls. Both are constructed like giant thermos bottles. Insulated and refrigerated, they are designed to carry vast quantities of supercold liquid natural gas (LNG) and liquid petroleum gas (LPG). Both gases are important sources of energy.

Natural gas comes from below the ground—sometimes by itself, sometimes in company with oil. Compressed under extremely low temperature

A more conventional liquid-gas tanker loads up
at a Persian Gulf port.

(-260 degrees Fahrenheit or -160 degrees Celsius), the gas forms a liquid, LNG. LPG, which has properties similar to LNG and is handled in much the same manner, is a by-product of refined oil.

When a liquid-gas tanker arrives at its destination, the cargo passes through a special warming facility that reconverts it into gas. One part of liquid expands into six hundred parts of gas. So great is this expansion that a single large liquid-

A liquid-gas tanker carries its cargo in giant
round thermos tanks.

gas tanker, making fifteen round trips from a LNG loading terminal in Algeria, could provide enough heating and cooking gas to support all of New England for a full year.

Thus, today's big ships have emerged. Giant single-superstructure bridge-aft vessels, they are nicknamed "stem-winders" because all of the action is in the stern. They are the modern tankers that now distribute vast quantities of oil and liquid gas to all major areas of the world.

3
BUILDING THE BIG SHIPS

Oil tankers have steadily grown in size until they are now the largest transport vehicles on Earth. One major reason for this growth is the soaring demand for petroleum throughout the world. Despite threatened shortages, consumption continues without letup.

The United States is the world's leading consumer of petroleum products by far. Every day each American man, woman, and child uses the amount of energy contained in three gallons of oil and several hundred cubic feet of natural gas. About half of this oil and an ever-increasing amount of gas, reduced to liquid form, is transported by tanker from the Middle East, Africa, Indonesia, Mexico, and Alaska.

Following the Arab-Israel Six-Day War in June, 1967, the Suez Canal was blocked by ships scuttled and sunk in midchannel. Thus, the short route between the oil-producing area of the Persian Gulf and the European markets no longer existed. Suddenly oil destined for Europe or for the east coast of North America had to be shipped an extra 9,000 miles around the southern tip of Africa. Weeks were added to each trip and put a great strain on tanker capacity. There were not enough ships to meet oil transportation demands.

Long, costly voyages added to the price of oil. (LNG was little used at the time.) Small tankers, which had been built to pass through the canals, became uneconomical over the much greater disstances. The pressing need was for bigger tankers that could deliver more oil in one trip around the Cape of Good Hope than a dozen or more small tankers could carry.

The age of the big ships had arrived. Fortunately, shipyards in many countries already had begun modifying their facilities in order to build larger tankers. Japan, in particular, with great shipyards that had escaped destruction during

38

World War II, quickly started the construction of jumbo tankships.

Even during the closing months of the war, Japan had been a leader in changing the design and construction methods for large, strong tankers. Though it now shares some of that leadership with other important shipbuilding nations, including the United States, Japan still produces many of the world's largest and most modern vessels.

Manufacturing tankers requires meticulous planning coupled with the best construction techniques. The main consideration during the entire process must be safety: safety for the crew, safety for the environment, and safety for the cargo.

During the planning phase, shipbuilder and customer determine the size and shape of the vessel. The size should be large and the shape simple and boxlike in order to carry maximum cargo.

Before a foot of steel is cut or a seam welded, the plan for every structural part of the ship is checked by computer for potential weak spots. After thousands of data bits are fed to the computer, the reading may indicate that an extra four-inch brace is needed here or a thicker gauge of steel is required there. In time, a complete model emerges from the many electronic readouts. But it's a mathematical model; it wouldn't float in a bathtub.

Once the design is complete, the shipyard begins the actual work. Most tankers are constructed in drydocks that can be flooded so the hull simply floats out when it is ready. Some vessels are built on the heavy timbers of waterside slipways and skidded into the water when the hull is seaworthy.

Great loads of steel arrive at the shipyard before construction begins. There are steel rods, steel beams, and stacks of steel plate, the vessel's main building blocks.

Deep in the drydock or on the ways, shipwrights start to construct the keel, the ship's foundation. A tanker keel is not laid in a single unit. It is formed out of beams that grow in length and strength as they are welded together.

While the first sections of keel are being put in

A steel sheet is swung into place.

place, the flat steel plates are laid out in nearby fabricating shops. Special machines tattoo computerized patterns on their surfaces. Batteries of cutting torches follow the patterns, producing an infinite number of designs. Certain of these pieces go to special hydraulic presses, which shape the plates into curved or rounded parts.

These jigsaw pieces of steel are then welded into sections. The welds are carefully X-rayed and

Prefabricated webs are manually fitted and welded to panels.

inspected, and where necessary stiffening bars, or bracing beams, are added. Single pieces are joined to form larger units.

Several coats of protective paint are applied to the unit before it is transported outside to the drydock and fitted into the tanker.

Piece by piece, the massive hull grows. Each unit, some the size of a house, welds to and strengthens the section to which it is assembled. Slowly the vessel takes shape.

The main strengthening members of a tanker run lengthwise along the hull (longitudinal) instead of crosswise (transverse) as is customary in heavily ribbed vessels. This structure is necessary because of the extreme length and weight of the tanker's boxlike hull. Strength is also provided by bulkheads and framing members, which divide the hull into separate tanks.

In a few months, the hull fills the drydock. Its gently curving bow is one of the last large pieces put into place. Most of the aft superstructure is complete, and the open deck seems to stretch to a distant horizon.

The ship's propeller is installed. Positioning the

A finished hull is ready to be floated
out of a drydock basin.

propeller shaft is a ticklish operation. If the shaft
is the least bit out of line, the ship will sail out of
trim. Extremely accurate laser-beam instruments
are used to place the propeller shaft in precise
fore-and-aft alignment.

Similarly, the massive rudder is hung on its
hinges beneath the stern.

Now the tanker looks like a ship, and it can
float. The gates to the low-level drydock are
opened. Water rushes in and fills the basin until
the vessel floats off the bottom.

The propeller and rudder

Tugboats coax a partially completed tanker
from the flooded drydock to a nearby fitting-out basin.

Since the engines have not yet been installed,
tugboats pull the new hull out of the basin and
nudge it alongside a nearby pier in the fitting-out
area. Many craftsmen go to work to outfit the
tanker for sea duty. Their collective job is to make
the vessel safe, functional, and comfortable.

Electricians run hundreds of miles of wiring
and hang fixtures. Plumbers set toilets and connect washbowls. Carpenters put in handrails and

cabinets. A stainless-steel galley is installed on a low deck of the superstructure. High up on the bridge, electronic specialists fix myriad radar-scopes and sophisticated navigational aids in place.

Lifeboats are hung on special davits and tested. Platforms from which giant rotating nozzles can sweep the deck with fire-fighting foam are strategically located on the main deck. Powerful windlasses are bolted to the foredeck plating. They reel in the chains that draw the massive anchors into place on each side of the bow. A spare anchor and a spare propeller are secured to the forecastle bulkhead and to an empty space on the deck.

As the fitting out of the ship continues, the deck becomes a maze of cargo pipelines, stripping lines for emptying the bottoms of the tanks, and bunkering lines for the ship's fuel. There are also water lines and lines to carry the fire-smothering foam. Long boxed-in trays filled with cables and electric wiring further clutter the deck.

Large and small valves, either hand-operated

or automated, are set into the piping. They will control the flow of liquid cargo. Like exposed metal viscera, this mass of deck accessories makes up a big part of the tanker's vital organs.

Winches, chocks, bitts, fairleads, and all the other deck paraphernalia needed to dock the ship are installed. Kingposts, still used to support loading booms, are raised. Up near the bow a battery of deck lights, a bell, and a foghorn are fastened to the foremast.

A tall mast rises above the roof of the wheelhouse far aft atop the superstructure. Several radar antennas, plus various other communications aerials, sprout from it. Under a large dome are the special antennas for the Marisat system (Marine satellite), the most advanced shipboard communications network ever developed.

Also attached to the mast is a lanyard used to hoist the internationally recognized signal flags that are neatly stacked inside the wheelhouse.

Chairs and beds, desks and dressers, refrigerators and television sets come aboard and are put in place while the ship lies anchored in the fitting-out basin.

A 265,000-dwt tanker undergoes outfitting.

However, the vessel hasn't really come alive yet, nor will it until the boilers, turbines, pumps, generators, water distillers, and complicated gearboxes are set up. One by one they are installed in the engine room. This area, called the "engine flat," is a vast cathedrallike chamber occupying the lower aft end of the ship. It extends several decks up into the superstructure and is packed full of all kinds of ship's machinery.

In due time everything is in place. Throughout the entire construction and fitting-out process the vessel has undergone continuous checks, tests, and inspections.

49

The day arrives when the tanker is ready for the open sea. Before it is commissioned, it makes a couple of trial runs. On the first, which may last for several days, the ship is peopled with the workmen who have built it. If something doesn't function properly during this time, an expert is on hand to fix it. This initial trial run may be a pleasure cruise or a headache, depending on how well the ship was put together.

The second trial run is for the officers and crew who will be operating the ship on its regular work schedule. Most have seen duty on similar tankers, but there are always some differences in a new vessel—perhaps updated instrumentation or equipment, or unusual running procedures.

Both officers and seamen acquaint themselves with the new ship and learn to function as a team. They will not always sail together—most tankermen rotate duties and change ships often—yet each must know what is expected of him or her in any situation or on any ship. Once the vessel is in the water, the success of each voyage depends upon the care and maintenance given it and the seamanship of those who sail it.

4
CARE AND CREW

The sea is a stern taskmaster
Never yielding
Sometimes quiet—
Always waiting.

Anonymous

Operating a tanker is an exacting job that involves many people with varied skills. It must be done with care; the sea does not forgive mistakes.

A tanker's business begins ashore. Scheduling, provision supply, and maintenance are handled by a shore-based transportation or marine department that represents the shipowner or operator. Most people in the department have years of sea duty behind them, and they are fully aware of government and international regulations regarding ship maintenance. They also know what fuel and supplies will be needed for each trip. They make periodic and thorough inspections of the vessel, both at sea and in port. They consult the captain, the first mate, and the chief engineer, who are responsible for the operation of the ship. They listen to the chief steward, whose job is the care and feeding of the crew. After each voyage, they read the detailed reports and the ship's log. These shore-based professionals also arrange for another tanker to move in when one vessel changes schedule or is temporarily out of service.

For safety's sake, and to keep the vessel in top working order, a tanker should enter a shipyard about every two years for an inspection and any needed repairs. Every four years, the ship should be put in drydock and checked thoroughly for structural weaknesses or corrosion. Major maintenance may be in order. The hull may need to be sandblasted and completely painted. New boilers may be needed in the engine room to replace those that are caked with mineral residue from the water. A propeller may be nicked and require

Tankers are repaired to insure safe sailing.

regrinding or replacing. Heavy wax and asphalt deposits may have to be manually scraped off tank walls. These jobs can be done best in a shipyard. In fact, the list of things to be done while the ship is in drydock may cover several single-spaced typewritten pages. Not until the last item is checked off is the tanker ready to put back to sea.

Working with the chief steward, the marine department supplies the ship with food, bedding, movies, and other stores required for the comfort and welfare of the officers and crew.

Food for a single voyage may include a thousand pounds of beef, pork, veal, and chicken. The supply coordinator may add fifty pounds of bananas, ninety pounds of tomatoes, twenty-five pounds of cookies, a dozen gallons of salad oil, and hundreds of small boxes of cereal. Crates of eggs, cases of cheese, barrels of milk, and bags of cold cuts go aboard. Coffee, the seaman's staff of life, is provided in unstinted amounts.

Normally, the tanker is fully provisioned while in port. However, on long voyages perishables may run out or other shortages occur. In those cases, the ship frequently is resupplied at sea by a small launch or helicopter. Most big tankers have a helicopter pad, usually a big circle marked on a clear area of the deck. It is particularly useful in the event of injury or illness that requires medical evacuation to a shoreside hospital.

Once at sea, the day-by-day operation and servicing of the tanker is entirely the responsibility of the officers and crew aboard the vessel. They are the ones who chart the course, steer the ship, coil the lines, set the tables, and keep the engines running.

A tanker crew usually numbers from twenty-five to forty men and women. The size of the crew depends on how updated and automated the tanker happens to be. About thirty-five people are needed to run a 250,000-dwt VLCC, and there may be additional cadets or officer trainees along.

Tanker crews are divided into three major divisions: deck, engineering, and steward. Though each has separate responsibilities, all hands work closely together as a team.

The vessel is under the direct command of the captain, or ship's master. Most captains receive much of their education at one of the several merchant-marine academies in the United States or abroad. Almost always captains command smaller vessels before they take over the bridge of a large tanker. Along with overseeing all operations of the ship, the captain has administrative duties—planning, record keeping, and supervision of all personnel.

Immediately under the captain's command are

several deck officers. The first officer, or chief mate, is his right-hand man. He is more concerned than anyone else with the actual operation of the ship. As much as the captain, who relies on him, the first mate needs to be aware of everything going on aboard ship. Usually found with a walkie-talkie radio in his hand, he stays in close communication with other officers and deck-hands.

There are at least two other mates aboard to share official duties. Like all officers, they have been trained for their positions and have spent

The navigating bridge is the focal point of the ship's operation.

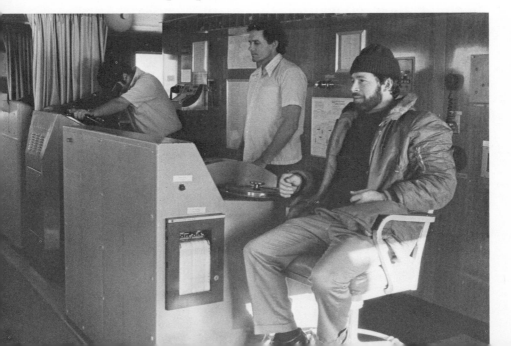

much time at sea. At least one mate always stands watch on the bridge with a helmsman, who is usually an able-bodied seaman. At night or in inclement weather, another seaman functions as a lookout on the bridgewing that stretches out on each side of the wheelhouse.

Captains and mates keep their skills updated by taking courses related to handling large tankers. One school in Grenoble, France, has a miniature water course over which officers can maneuver scale-model tankers to practice the delicate art of sailing and docking. Officers may also sail a simulator located in a converted aircraft hangar at La Guardia Field in New York.

At similar training facilities around the globe video-tape machines project moving displays of what is encountered when a ship enters any of several busy ports. From a life-sized replica of a tanker's bridge, the trainee maneuvers the ship through traffic and deals with emergency situations presented to him by computers. Simulators permit trainees to practice ship handling without risk to life, damage to environment, or danger to vessels.

Tanker officers train in simulators that electronically duplicate the problems encountered in busy ports.

A radio officer, invariably called Sparks, is an extremely important member of the crew. The radio shack is located on or near the bridge deck, and it is manned around the clock. Communication is a vessel's lifeline, and modern tankers carry highly sophisticated radio, telephone, and teletype systems.

One of the most modern shipboard maritime communications networks is called Marisat. Marisat uses three communications relay satellites

(Comsat) that circle the Earth in synchronous orbits some 23,000 miles out in space. (A synchronous orbit is one that matches the speed of the Earth's rotation, making the satellite appear to be standing still over a particular area of the Earth's surface.) Positioned over the Pacific, Atlantic, and Indian oceans, these satellites scan most of the world, beaming signals between each other as well as relaying them back and forth to Earth.

A radio operator

By means of Marisat, fast, reliable, high-quality voice or electronic messages reach ships at sea and shore points around the world. Along with other communications systems, it forms the crucial link between the parties concerned with the progress or problems of the vessel and its cargo. On many ships, Sparks is a woman.

Nonrated members of the deck department do most of the physical work aboard ship. This group consists largely of ordinary seamen (OS) and able-bodied seamen (AB). To become a seaman, a man or woman does not need a formal education or previous sea experience. However, an applicant for a job with the American Merchant Marine must get a letter of commitment from someone willing to give him or her a trial. That letter usually is earned by a show of interest, a willingness to work, and at least an average ability to accept orders and learn basic seamanship. Having obtained such a letter, the applicant presents it to the United States Coast Guard, which interviews and tests him or her.

After passing Coast Guard requirements, the applicant receives something called a "Z-card"

Maintenance keeps crew members busy.

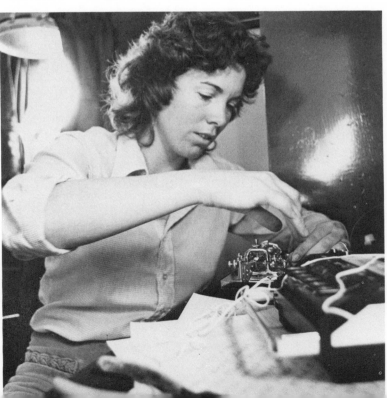

and thereby becomes an ordinary seaman. When he has spent at least a year of deck time at sea, usually performing the more menial tasks, an OS is eligible to take further Coast Guard tests for a limited AB rating. If he completes another three years on deck, the experienced young mariner rates a green ticket as a full-fledged AB.

Also after three years of deck duty, a person may apply for a third mate's rating, thereby moving up to officer's rank. There is no reason why a seaman cannot come up the ladder and in time become a captain. Most petroleum and shipping companies offer promising candidates the opportunity to study at a qualified merchant-marine academy and then a period of apprenticeship at sea.

The mechanical operation and maintenance of the ship are the responsibility of the engineering department. The chief engineer needs mechanical skills and plenty of sea experience. His crew of assistant engineering officers and several enginemen keep the powerful turbines or diesel engines running and the propeller turning. The engineering department also operates the com-

An engineer checks lubrication of the spinning
propeller shaft.

plicated cargo pumps located deep down near the
ship's bilge. Engineers tend the desalinators, or
distillers, that supply all the fresh water used on
the ship. They oversee all the machinery aboard
the vessel.

The steward is charged with the care and feeding of the ship's crew. The job is an important

one, for an unsatisfied crew makes for an unhappy tanker. A chief steward supervises one or more cooks and bakers plus several messpersons. Beyond seeing that the seamen are properly fed, the steward and his personnel supply officers and seamen with towels, clean linen, and other comforts and necessities of life at sea. They also keep the vessel clean and shipshape.

Regardless of which department a tankerman or tankerwoman works in, each stands two watches during a twenty-four-hour day. Each watch is four hours long, and there are eight hours between watches. For instance, the person stand-

The ship's galley

ing the eight-to-noon watch also stands the eight-to-midnight watch. Other watches are twelve-to-four, and four-to-eight.

Deckhands often are called upon to work longer than a regular watch. During docking and un-docking operations, most crew members are needed on deck to handle the winches, run the lines, and perform numerous other tasks in preparation for loading or discharging cargo. On most ships, and certainly on American-flag ships, over-time is paid those who work beyond their normal four-hour watch. At sea or in port, important service and maintenance functions may also war-rant overtime.

Officers and seamen usually spend long periods at sea. Some tankers virtually never touch land, but load and discharge cargoes at special mooring buoys located miles away from shore. Others spend days at sea for each hour spent alongside a dock. Even then off-duty members of the crew seldom bother to go ashore. Oil usually is loaded at remote and desolate sites that offer few scenic attractions. And the time needed to load or dis-charge a cargo of oil often is too short to do much

Crew members occupy comfortable private quarters.

in. Most crew members stay aboard, make use of the library, watch movies or video-tape television shows, play Ping Pong, pump iron in the small gym, swim if there is a pool aboard, and eat. There always is food available.

66

Some ships allow wives to accompany their officer husbands. This practice helps combat the loneliness that is a part of tankering.

After lengthy stretches of sea duty, tanker officers and crew enjoy extended paid vacations ashore, lasting several weeks to a couple of months at a time. Their air fare home is also paid.

When they return to sea, deck officers and crew members often are assigned to a different tanker. Thus, a constant rotation of personnel takes place. Officers and seamen must regularly adapt to unfamiliar ships and work with new crew members. Since tankers are basically the same, such changes create no problems. Over the years, tankermen's paths cross and recross, and there are plenty of tales to tell of experiences they have had in distant corners of the world since they were last together.

5
ACCIDENTS, SPILLS AND SAFETY

Like trucks, trains, and cargo-carrying air-planes, oil tankers get into accidents. Considering the billions of tons of cargo they move, tanker safety records compare favorably with those of other carriers. But a major tanker wreck is set apart from the accidents of other vehicles because of the terrible consequences. Few things anger the average citizen more than a photograph of a seabird mired in the muck of an oil spill. A beach covered with black ooze is not soon forgotten.

However, tankers must sail, and because of their numbers on sea-lanes and crowded water-ways, there always will be the risk of accidents. The challenge is to limit the damage as much as possible.

There are many causes of tanker mishaps. An aging or carelessly loaded ship may crack a seam in a rough sea and spill oil. A tanker may suddenly lose power, drift helplessly onto the rocks, and break up. An empty or partially filled tank that has not been properly protected with inert gas may explode. The causes are many, and the most common is human error—a misread chart, an unnecessary risk, a navigational blunder, an inadequately trained officer or seaman.

Most large oil-dealing countries have special arms of government specifically charged with the enforcement of maritime regulations. The Ministry of Transport in Canada, the Department of Trade in Britain, and the Maritime Safety Agency of Japan are agencies that function to assure that all ships operating in their waters abide by the laws.

Individual governments also are aided by international societies such as the Intergovernmental Maritime Consultive Organization (IMCO). With approximately one hundred member nations, IMCO formulates international agreements to improve life at sea, regulate vessel traffic on

congested sea-lanes, prevent oil pollution, and en-
sure that parties responsible for spills clean up the
mess and pay for any damage and restoration.
Threatened by massive fines or dismissal, any
ship's master would think twice before dumping
oily waste at sea.

In the United States, the Federation of American Controlled Shipping (FACS), an association
of American ship users who own or charter foreign-flag ships, have tightened inspections on
these ships operating in or out of United States
ports.

The Coast Guard is the primary Government
agency charged with controlling ship traffic, en-
forcing safety rules, and dealing with pollution
in United States territorial waters and inland
waterways. Under Coast Guard surveillance, both
American-registered and foreign-flag ships abide
by strict rules when in United States coastal
waters. The Coast Guard is empowered to board
and regularly inspect all vessels entering or operating within territorial waters. It levies fines on
any ship that ignores or bends the rules. Flagrant
or repeated abuses are sufficient cause to deny a

A grounded oil barge

ship entry into protected waters. If inspections reveal unsafe or unclean practices, the vessel can be ordered out of port.

The Coast Guard sees that ships carry updated charts and have efficient navigation, communication, and safety equipment aboard. To prevent accidents, it controls the movement of traffic. A ship must stay within established sea-lanes and

71

maintain safe clearance from any other vessels in the area. When one ship encroaches upon another's path, an identifying blip flashes on the radarscope of the tanker's collision-avoidance system, which immediately sounds a warning and works out a safe course of evasive action by computer.

The Coast Guard also requires that any tanker over 20,000-dwt capacity be equipped with an inert-gas (I.G.) system. This system is a large, complicated maze of machinery and plumbing that takes spent flue gas from the ship's stack, cleans it, and forces it into the empty cargo-tank space. Having had virtually all of its oxygen burned away in the boiler, the waste inert gas will not support combustion, so tank fires or explosions cannot occur.

The newer big tankers have extra boiler or spare engines in case the primary power plant should fail. Such backup propulsion systems are not powerful enough to keep the tanker sailing on its scheduled run, but they do provide enough emergency horsepower to enable the ship to get into some shipyard for repair.

Most new tankers also carry an extra generator or alternator. Without electricity a tanker becomes a helpless derelict, wallowing in the sea without rudder power, communications, operating navigation instruments, or most other necessities.

Each of these many systems must be regularly inspected and serviced to prevent serious problems at sea. Responsible tanker owners and operators practice such preventive maintenance. Furthermore, the Coast Guard can use its authority to demand that the work be done or deny the ship use of territorial waters or entry into port. Such Coast Guard vigilance causes most substandard vessels to avoid United States ports. Tanker charterers prefer not to hire ships with bad reputations for fear that their cargoes will not be allowed to enter American harbors.

But transporting oil is an international activity. A relatively small percentage of it is done in American-built, American-owned, American-crewed ships. Most tankers are privately owned, foreign built, sail under foreign flags, and are operated by foreign crews. The reasons are largely economical. With cheaper labor and fewer restrictions, it costs less to build a tanker in Japan, Spain, or Holland than it does in the United States. A tanker that is licensed and registered in Liberia or Panama pays fewer taxes and fees than are required of an American-flag ship. Also, foreign seamen receive less pay than the unionized members of American crews.

It can be argued that cutting economic corners tends to reduce the quality and safety of a ship's operation. Foreign-flag ships do figure in many more accidents and pollution violations, perhaps because there are many more foreign-flag tankers at sea and they make longer and more hazardous voyages. Where to place the major blame for tanker mishaps is difficult to know, but close inspections, safety equipment, improved crew training, and more forceful policing are helping to bring about a reduction.

The accidents that do happen usually involve aging tankers which should have been taken out of service long before. Tankers deteriorate under the steady pounding of the sea. The acids in their petroleum cargoes slowly erode their steel plating. Their boilers cake up, engines wear out, and instruments begin to malfunction. Generally a ten- or fifteen-year-old tanker is approaching the end of its usefulness.

Too often these tankers are given a minimum of servicing and kept at sea beyond their normal life-span. Most are low-tonnage vessels, but their large numbers compared to VLCCs and ULCCs create a dangerous traffic hazard. And even the smallest tanker can cause a devastating spill. Although extra policing is directed toward controlling such rust buckets, once on the high seas a careless captain has ample opportunity to bend the rules.

A classic example of this problem occurred in December, 1976. The *Argo Merchant*, an aging 28,000-dwt tanker, ran onto a shoal in international waters some thirty miles from Nantucket Island, off the coast of Massachusetts. Slowly breaking up, it spilled seven and a half million gallons of fuel oil into the Atlantic Ocean.

The *Argo Merchant* already had a dubious reputation. Not only did it have a history of pollution violations, but its navigational gear was suspected to be faulty. Even the skillfulness of its crew was questionable. In all, the *Merchant* was not considered seaworthy. The United States Coast Guard was prepared to board and inspect the vessel as soon as it arrived in United States territorial waters and no longer enjoyed the immunity of the high seas.

But the *Argo Merchant* never got close enough to the mainland to come under Coast Guard jurisdiction. Instead of being able to check it out,

The Coast Guard comes to the rescue of the *Argo Merchant's* crew.

the Coast Guard suddenly found itself charged with rescuing the ship's crew. The tanker was lost, but its crew was saved. At least, the millions of gallons of spilled fuel oil was dissipated in the stormy sea and never polluted the shore.

Accidents can also happen to new and skillfully crewed ships. On the evening of March 16, 1978, the modern, well-operated tanker *Amoco Cadiz*, a 220,000-dwt VLCC, lost steering power off the coast of Brittany. Despite frantic efforts to get towing lines on the ship, it drifted relentlessly onto the coastal rocks. Within a few days it broke up and spilled a horrendous fifty million gallons of oil into the ocean.

The oozing black tide spread more than a hundred miles along the coast of France and extended a dozen miles out to sea. It took a heavy toll of seabirds and marine life. Particularly hard hit were the commercial beds that had provided France with its major supply of oysters. Tourism to Brittany's once-fine beaches was ruined for the coming season. To date, the wrecking of the *Amoco Cadiz* has been the world's worst pollution disaster.

The Coast Guard investigates a burning oil platform.

On New Year's Eve, 1978, the Greek tanker *Andros Patria* exploded and caught fire off the coast of Spain. Thirty-four people who abandoned ship into stormy seas were lost; more than fifteen million gallons of oil were spilled.

The most tragic accident of all occurred just a week later. On January 7, 1979, the French tanker *Betelgeuse*, a 120,000-ton ship, was moored to a jetty about three miles offshore of Bantry, Ireland. It was discharging its cargo through undersea pipes to a shoreside terminal. Suddenly two blasts ripped through the vessel, cutting it in two and hurling bodies into a sea of flaming oil. Fifty lives were lost. Had the partially emptied tanks been properly topped off with oxygen-free inert gas, the tragedy might have been averted.

Any tanker accident demands fast action to limit environmental damage. When a spill occurs offshore and oil washes onto a beach, everyone available is needed to help clean it up. Straw, hay, and certain polyurethane materials make fine blotters. Where feasible, attempts are made to vacuum up the oil or skim it off the water before it can reach shore.

Because all tankers have their hulls divided into numerous small cargo tanks, a ruptured or beached vessel may start leaking oil from only one or two of its tanks. Great effort is then made to pump out the oil from the other tanks before

A grounded tanker blackens a Puerto Rican beach with oil.

the ship breaks up completely, which not only prevents major pollution, but salvages much valuable oil.

If a spill occurs far out at sea, the floating blanket sometimes is ignited to consume the oil before it spreads. Success depends largely upon how calm the water happens to be.

It was once thought that the world's oceans were so vast and chemically active that they could break up, dissolve, purify, or simply hide all the rubbish discharged into them. People now know that this idea is not true. Any body of water can absorb only so much unwanted material before it becomes unhealthy or even dies. Fortunately, if the offending materials are removed or no longer allowed into the water, in most instances nature heals the wounds and health eventually returns.

Even after a disastrous oil spill, water clears and tarry beaches whiten and again become habitable. Wild birds return, and marine life recovers. Slowly bacterial action of seaborne microorganisms breaks down and then dissolves the molecules of oil.

Most spills occur at dockside or close to shore. A large percentage of spillage takes place at the terminal where oil is being loaded or discharged —a hose may break, a valve may crack, a seal may rupture and spray high-pressure streams of oil into the surrounding water. Fortunately, most such spills can be quickly traced and stopped.

Often a floating barrier, or containment boom, is strung out around the tanker to prevent a spill from spreading. When the leak has been fixed,

Floating barriers help prevent a minor oil spill
from spreading.

the oil inside the boom is pumped out or skimmed
off the water and saved.

There are several ways to handle tanker mishaps and oil pollution, and more are being developed. But the best method by far is to prevent
accidents, and responsibile oil companies and
tanker operators are concentrating on such pre-
vention.

6
ON THE HIGH SEAS

Before a tanker can leave port to take on a new load of oil, it must first empty its tanks of its last cargo. Powerful pumps deep within the docked vessel suck out the final barrels of oil.

The pumped-out crude passes through the maze of valves and pipes that crisscross the tanker's deck. It leaves the ship through the articulated pipes of the chicksan, which is a hinged apparatus that automatically adjusts to any movement of the docked vessel. The I.G. system fills the empty tank space with inert gas to prevent the possibility of fire or explosion.

As the last of the cargo leaves the ship, the tanker is flying light and ready to leave. It is time to set sail to pick up another load of crude. Officers and crew report to their posts; if the vessel is berthed in a harbor, a pilot may come aboard to navigate the ship.

Before the empty tanker reaches open water, it takes in a few thousand tons of seawater ballast to settle it a bit deeper and help keep it stable in a rolling, pitching sea. Without ballast, the high-riding tanker would be inclined to twist, vibrate, and bend dangerously.

Insofar as possible, ballast is carried in special segregated tanks. Near the end of the voyage, this clean ballast can be pumped into the sea without danger of pollution.

En route, the tanker usually takes on some dirty ballast as well. Dirty ballast often is composed of tank washings. Empty cargo tanks require periodic cleaning, because paraffin, which separates out of the crude oil, clings to the tank sides. Some of the oil itself, perhaps mixed with sand, also builds up a deposit. Most modern tankers use permanently installed automatic tank-washing machines to knock the gummy residue from the tank walls. Remotely controlled pivoting nozzle turrets located in the depths of each tank direct high-pressure streams of liquid onto the walls. If water is used, the oily washings are retained aboard and form part of the ship's ballast. Although clean ballast may be discharged anywhere at sea, contaminated ballast must be treated before it can be disposed of.

If the outward voyage is long enough, the oil in the dirty ballast rises to the top and the clear water settles to the bottom. When the time comes, the water is discharged from beneath the oil, and

A 265,000-dwt VLCC, empty and high in the water

the oil is retained and combined with the next cargo. This procedure is known as the load-on-top (LOT) system and is used by a large percentage of today's tankers.

Often the tank-cleaning nozzles use oil to remove the residue, not unlike an auto mechanic who cleans the grease from his hands by washing them in oil. The oil simply comes from the cargo.

Even under ballast, a tanker with empty cargo tanks rides high in the water. A large tanker may draw a mere seventeen feet of water—its draft—near the lightened bow. But at the aft end, the weight of the heavy superstructure, engine-room machinery, full fuel-oil tanks, massive rudder and propeller may sink the stern thirty feet or more into the water. Depending on its size, each ship has a different draft, which determines what ports it can safely enter or what waterways it can sail. (Draft is easily determined by a numbered scale marked plainly on a vessel's hull.) There are no rivers or canals and scarcely any port in the United

The depth of a ship's draft
is carefully marked on its hull.

MOBILOIL

38
37
36
35
34
33
32
31
30
29
28
27
26
25
24
23
22
21
20
19
18
17
16
15
14
13
12
11
10
9

States that can handle a ship with more than a forty-five-foot draft. In those places smaller ships are used or the size of the cargo reduced.

While at sea, the captain, one or two mates, and a helmsman navigate and sail the vessel from the bridge deck high atop the superstructure. Modern tankers are so automated that only two people are needed to stand watch on the bridge during much of the voyage. Their duty largely is that of monitoring instruments that tell what the ship is doing. Yet manual controls are always within reach. On a center console is a short throttle lever, or joystick, used to increase or decrease engine power. Next to it is a helmsman's wheel, a miniature of the six-foot spoked wheels of the early windjammers. Both controls are directly linked to the engine room. On most modern ships, the officer no longer has to turn a pointer to telegraph instructions to the engine room.

Close to the control console is at least one hooded radarscope. Usually there are two, each with its own scanning range. One scope may display objects within a twelve-mile radius of the ship while the other may reach out fifty miles.

On a mast high above the wheelhouse, the steadily rotating antennas sweep their beams over the water. Day or night, in fog or storm, radar paints an electronic picture that shows all land masses, shipping activity, or heavy weather in the vicinity of the vessel. Nearby is the computer-controlled collision-avoidance system and its radarscope that warns of any traffic hazard.

An array of precise electronic navigational equipment is located on the bridge or within the adjacent chartroom. In addition, all tankers carry a simple sextant. Weather and visibility permitting, the captain or one of the mates will often remove the sextant from its varnished case and shoot the stars to work out a fix of the vessel's position. It is good practice; if power to operate the sophisticated electronic systems should ever fail, the simple hand-held sextant used by Magellan and Columbus might mean survival.

Under way, captain and officers pore over maps and charts and work out a course by dead reckoning. They are aided by navigation satellite systems, gyrocompasses, autopilots, and other space-age equipment. Also, they are in constant

The ship's course is plotted in the chartroom.

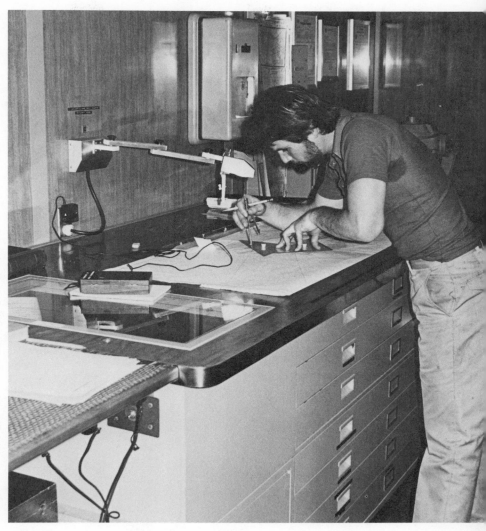

The Marisat dome and other antenna

communication with land stations and seaborne traffic. Given all these aids, only extreme carelessness or total instrument failure could cause a tanker to lose its way at sea.

But a disaster could happen. To be ready, safety drills are held during every voyage. Seven short blasts and one long one from the klaxon horn sound the general alarm to abandon ship. Crewmen pull on life jackets and scurry for the life-

Lifeboat drill

boats. Each man or woman has a specific task to perform. Some climb the davits and prepare to lower the boats; someone tests the engine; another makes sure provisions are in place; still another grabs a safety light and an automatic radio beacon.

When everything is checked out, each lifeboat is lowered partway over the side. That's enough. To lower the boats into the sea would mean a costly delay. So everyone waits for the all-clear signal, secure in the knowledge that the lifeboats are in working order and glad that the emergency is not a real one.

On another day, a fire drill is called. The ship's bell clangs, or the klaxon brays. Seamen jerk life vests from wall hooks, slip into them on the run, and hurry to their assigned fire-fighting posts. Some grab extinguishers. Others rush across the rolling deck, take their stations at fire-foam monitors, and aim water across the deck. During fire drills, the monitors are hooked to water pumps in order to save the foam retardant for a real emergency.

Everyone on the bridge is familiar with the

Foam cannons spew water during a fire drill.

action to take if a crewman falls overboard. There are no quick brakes on a tanker. Empty or full, a big ship requires several miles of sea room and probably twenty minutes to come to a stop. An emergency crash stop is accomplished by pulling the throttle back to "full astern," to reverse the

94

propeller, and putting the rudder hard over to one side.

In the event of a man overboard, however, the ship would be some distance from the distressed person when the vessel finally comes to a stop. So an overboard seaman is rescued by a maneuver known as the Williamson turn. Upon hearing the three long blasts from the ship's whistle that signal man overboard, the helmsman spins the wheel hard over so the tanker turns toward the side from which the crewman fell. This action swings the stern and the dangerous propeller away from the person in the water.

When the ship has turned sixty degrees off its original heading, the helmsman spins the wheel sharply in the opposite direction. He holds it there, maintaining speed, until the vessel has turned a full 180 degrees and reversed its course. Upon completing the loop, the tanker should be in sight of the swimming crewman and the rescue detail is already lowering the lifeboat to pick him up. In frigid arctic or shark-infested waters, the rescue maneuver has even greater urgency.

To be sure that no ship's call for help is unheard,

radio officers of all large vessels abide by an international agreement to hold a three-minute period of silence twice every hour of the day. Each hour, between the minutes of fifteen to eighteen and forty-five to forty-eight, all ships stop transmitting, turn their receivers to the 500 kilahertz frequency, and listen for distress signals. In this way they can pick up any ship's emergency call or the SOS from the hand-cranked portable transmitter carried aboard lifeboats.

There are few people more concerned with each other's safety than seafarers. Nor are there many who will drop what they are doing more quickly to go to the aid of another.

In order to minimize potential emergencies, a lot of maintenance work is done on the ship while it is at sea. Most takes place while sailing empty, when the vessel rides high in the water with its weather deck clear of the crashing seas.

Painting is a never-ending chore. Even the new paints that purportedly last forever give way to the salty corrosion of the sea. Rust pops through, paint powders and flakes off. So there always is plenty of scraping, sanding, and spotting to be done. Most tankers carry a supply of spare paint in the storage space beneath the forecastle deck.

Frayed cables require repairing, too. Hawser ropes need to be spliced, and empty tanks have to be inspected. Leaky valves are checked out and repaired. The time is rare when a person standing watch cannot find something to do. The activity is all to the good, for time can hang heavy on a long voyage.

Tankers of the world sail under many different flags, and their crews speak many different languages. But they all share the same duties and face the same problems. In order to survive, they must work diligently to keep their vessel safe and shipshape.

7
PICKUP
AND DELIVERY

In order to make a reasonable profit, a tanker must take on cargo and head out to sea as quickly as possible. Once in port and hooked up to the loading hoses or chicksan pipes, the ship immediately starts filling its tanks. Every safety precaution is taken. Tools that might strike sparks are put away. Only sealed flashlights are allowed on the deck. No one carries a lighter. Smoking is totally forbidden at all times outside of certain dining and living areas within the superstructure.

Throughout the night and most of the next day, the oil pours into the ship at a rate of perhaps twenty thousand tons an hour. Slowly the vessel sinks deeper and deeper into the water. In the cargo control room, the pumpman flips various switches studding a large tabletop display that diagrams the ship's tanks, valves, and cargo-handling lines. From this central console he can open or close cargo valves, start or stop pumps, and control the loading of the ship.

The pumpman keeps in close contact with the first mate, who works with a special computer that helps determine how the ship should be loaded to maintain proper trim. Overloading the center tanks can cause a ship to crack in rough seas. Failing to balance the amount of crude oil carried in the wing tanks along the port and starboard

A tanker operates day and night.

sides of the hull can cause the ship to wrench its seams or twist dangerously in a rolling sea. Some twisting tolerance is built into a tanker, just as it is built into the flexible wings of a commercial airliner.

Looking out along the deck of a tanker in heavy seas, one is amazed to see the steel deck writhe and toss in rhythm with the water. Only if the motion becomes excessive does the ship slow down.

When sailing empty, the tanker may show some fifty feet of hull above the water. Now, when it is filled, the amount of freeboard is about twenty feet. Four-fifths of the hull is out of sight. Someone goes ashore to check the Plimsoll mark, which consists of horizontal lines painted on the side of the vessel. They indicate the maximum load level for safe travel during winter or summer, in cold or tropical waters, or in fresh water. To load beyond the appropriate Plimsoll mark is to invite trouble and can cause the cancellation of the insurance on the vessel.

When the tanks are topped off, some spare room is left to accommodate any expansion the crude

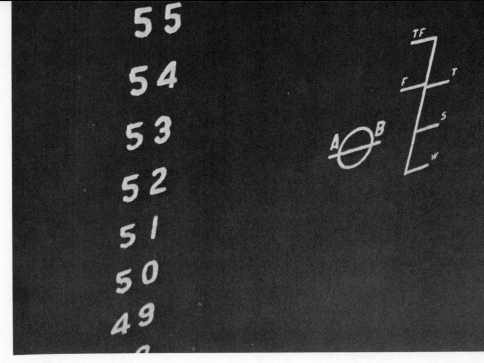

The depth-of-draft scale (left)
and the Plimsoll mark (right)

oil may undergo during its voyage through warm waters. This empty space is called "ullage."

When the tanks are fully loaded, seamen begin disconnecting the large hoses or chicksan pipes in preparation for departure. If the tanker has been loading at a shore installation, one of the seamen is assigned to search the ship and make a careful nose count of the crew. Weeks, indeed months, may pass before the tanker or any other vessel of

101

the company's fleet returns to that particular port. Being left behind at some remote desert or arctic loading station is like being abandoned on the moon . . . without pay.

As the cargo lines are disconnected, the harbor pilot comes aboard and takes his station on the navigation bridge. The tugboats pull alongside

The oil passes through a hinging pipe assembly called a "chicksan."

Tugboats aid a tanker in and out of port.

and toot their readiness. Deckhands and dock workers cast off mooring lines.

Following walkie-talkie directions from the pilot, the tugs slowly ease the tanker away from the loading pier. They team up to nudge and pull the vessel fore and aft, turning it until the bow points toward the open sea.

At the harbor exit the pilot descends a rope-laced ladder onto the bobbing deck of a small pilot boat. The tugs give a farewell toot and turn back.

"Full ahead," the captain instructs the deck officer at the control console.

"Full ahead." The mate eases the throttle lever another notch forward.

"Bearing one nine seven."

"One nine seven," the helmsman responds, turning the small wheel and watching the compass needle swing to the correct heading.

The tanker moves like a water-soaked log into the open sea. Its blunt bow pushes through the swells instead of riding over them. As the vessel shoulders its way through the turbulent seas, the deck is often awash with white water flung high by the low-plunging bow. It rushes foaming across the deck, sloshes back and forth with the roll of

A fully loaded tanker sails low in the water.

the ship, then drains overboard as the next roily swell comes boiling over the rail. No one is injured, for during a severe storm, seamen sensibly stay within the superstructure.

Every loose item or piece of deck equipment has been lashed down or safely stowed away in the forecastle. Still, accidents happen. Seamen tell many stories of the havoc raised by an object that comes loose during a storm. On one occasion, an insecurely bolted forty-ton spare propeller tore loose in a heavy sea. As crewmen watched helplessly from the safety of the superstructure, the propeller slid wildly back and forth over the deck. It uprooted mooring bitts and fairleads, crashed into several winches, leveled tank hatches, and made twisted wreckage of the deck piping. Not until the deck was swept clean did the propeller finally crash through the railing and sink out of sight. Usually, however, a tanker is able to operate safely in any weather.

Most tankers sail according to a plan, but sometimes plans go awry. A tanker captain is not always sure where his cargo will end up. He may be far at sea when his radio officer brings him a

A tanker in heavy seas

message to change course and discharge all or part of his oil at an unscheduled port.

Usually, no particular problems result from such deviations. Inconveniences can be taken care of en route. If food is running low, or other important items are needed, a small launch or helicopter may be chartered to deliver the needed supplies when the diverted tanker sails within a reasonable distance of shore.

The large number of tankers at sea and their changing schedules sometimes cause overcrowding of shipping lanes. For the sake of safety, careful control of their movements must be maintained. The Dover Strait, the narrow waist of the English Channel that separates Great Britain from France, often becomes clogged with ships of all kinds. Many are mammoth tankers, carrying crude oil from Saudi Arabia around the southern tip of Africa to major European ports. Traffic through the Strait is further complicated by ferries and small craft sailing directly across the tanker lanes. The danger of collision is always present.

The Strait of Malacca between the island of Sumatra and the Malay Peninsula has the width to accommodate many ships, but it is dangerously shallow. Only a single narrow channel is deep enough for very large tankers. Vessels loaded down with Kuwaiti crude oil jockey for position in the narrow strip.

Even the wide Strait of Gibraltar becomes overcrowded at times with large and small ships all going in various directions.

Precise traffic patterns and safety rules are usually carefully maintained in these busy shipping lanes. However, reckless or irresponsible captains, eager to insure themselves a berth, occasionally try to break the rules. Fortunately, most of these men soon find themselves "on the beach" without a ship, which helps to upgrade the quality of both officers and seamen sailing today's tankships.

There is also international cooperation to establish safe sailing practices for tankers. Sea-lanes are carefully separated to reduce the chance of collision between southbound and northbound vessels. The accepted practice is for ships to pass

The world's major tanker routes

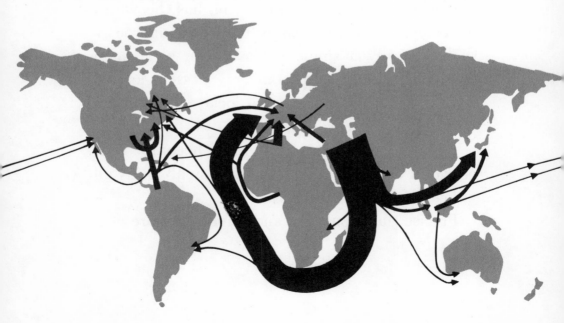

to the right, or starboard, of each other. At times this may vary, however. For instance, when the route lies close to shore, the empty ship often passes on the land side, allowing the cargo-filled tanker lots of sea room in deep water. In case of accident, the farther out the laden ship is the less chance there is of any spilled oil reaching the beach.

All ships, of course, should be kept well informed of sailing or navigational variations from charts. Coast-guard units of different nations or other planning and policing agencies establishing sea routes, set up traffic-control procedures, and watch over shipping operations in order to prevent accidents.

Still another safeguard exists in the fact that the number of tankers has steadily decreased in almost direct proportion to their increase in size. As a result, chances for accidents and collisions are greatly reduced.

Thus, with bigger and better ships, improved regulations, international concern and cooperation, and stricter enforcement, tankers are sailing more safely and cleanly than ever before.

8
UNLOADING

The final and probably most important part of an oil tanker's mission is to discharge its cargo. Though the operation may seem simple, the procedure is complicated and a mistake can be costly.

Most of today's crude oil is moved around the world in 200,000- to 300,000-dwt VLCCs. The even-larger ULCCs are also transporting more all the time. But the big ships have their problems. As they draw from sixty to ninety feet of water when fully loaded, there are few ports that can handle them. The ones that can, approximately 150, are spread thinly around the globe. Luckily, most are close to densely populated regions where oil and petroleum products are most needed.

Ship traffic in and out of these major deepwater

ports is heavy. A big tanker often has to wait its turn to enter such places as Yokahama, Japan; Genoa, Italy; Wilhelmshaven, Germany; or Rotterdam, in the Netherlands.

Long before reaching port, the tanker radios ahead to see if a berth will be available when it

A moderate-size tanker at an Alaskan berth

arrives. It may send its estimated time of arrival (ETA) when still three days out at sea. It will send again in two days, and once more on the final day, hoping that the port authorities will have prepared a place.

If the facilities are overcrowded, the captain may have to reduce speed and kill a little time while the ship ahead finishes unloading and moves away from the terminal. If the delay is to be lengthy, the incoming ship may have to drop anchor offshore until the captain gets clearance to enter the harbor. Such delays are costly and worrisome.

When clearance arrives, the indispensable harbor pilot comes aboard. Well-versed in the currents, tides, shoreline, and bottom hazards of the area, he guides the ship to its mooring.

"Forty ahead," the pilot calls from the bridge wing.

"Forty ahead." The mate at the engine throttle pulls back on the black joystick to reduce propeller revolutions to forty rpm's. They enter the harbor slowly.

"Hard right."

"Hard right." The helmsman spins the wheel hard over.

"Ease to ten."

"Ease to ten."

"Steady."

A team of tugboats emerge from the darkness. Their running lights glow in the night, and powerful searchlights atop their wheelhouses sweep the tanker's sides and splash light upon the low deck.

"Dead slow," instructs the pilot. The tanker's propeller barely turns.

The most delicate part of the docking operation now takes place. Miscalculating the speed of the heavily laden ship could crunch the pier or put a gash in the tanker's steel plate. The tugboats coax the tanker along inch by inch, following the pilot's detailed walkie-talkie directions, and nestle it against the pier with a feather-light touch.

The tugs continue to press the tanker firmly against the dock until all the mooring cables and hawsers have been strung out and so arranged that the tanker is secured yet able to move upward or downward with the tide while it is being emptied.

When the vessel is winched in, the unloading hoses or chicksan pipes are hooked up and the pumps started as soon as possible. Meanwhile, a floating containment boom is towed into place as a precaution against any possible spill. Seamen check the valves and gaskets and patrol the pipes, looking for leaks.

Two or three days and several watches may be needed to empty the VLCC (even longer for a ULCC), but finally the last of the oil goes ashore.

A protective spill-containment boom encircles the tanker.

The tanker rides high once again. Preparations are already under way to undock, turn around, and go back for another load.

Where coastal deepwater ports are not available, other types of facilities have been developed. Some countries have built jetties that extend to where the water is deep enough for the big ships. When a tanker ties up, its cargo is pumped ashore through great pipes laid along the jetty.

At other locations, man-made deepwater islands, not unlike offshore oil-drilling platforms, accommodate the VLCCs and ULCCs. Pipes laid along the seabed carry the petroleum ashore.

Still another means to discharge oil is the single-point mooring system, commonly referred to as a monobuoy. Monobuoys have been around for years, but one of the newest, and the first real deep-water oil-discharging facility in the United States, is the Louisiana Offshore Oil Port, known as LOOP.

The basic element in the LOOP system is a large buoy firmly anchored in 100 feet of water about nineteen miles out in the Gulf of Mexico. Approximately the size of a four-story building with three stories below water, the monobuoy is attached to the bottom of the Gulf by a large underwater chain. The chain is fastened to a base structure, which has connections to transfer oil from the unloading hoses to the submarine pipeline that carries it to shore.

A specially trained mooring master boards the tanker when it is five miles from the unloading complex. He guides the ship to its berth at one of the several mooring buoys that make the LOOP system. The ship is moored by bowlines only and

A VLCC at a deep-water mooring platform

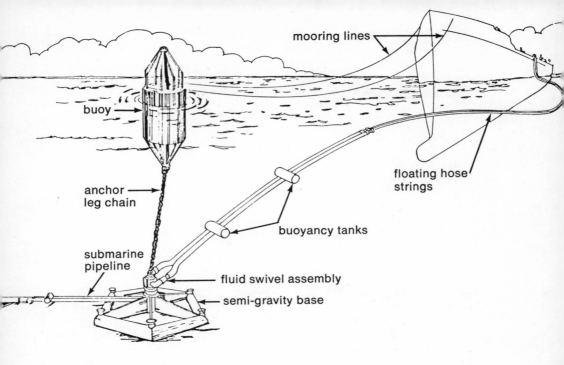

mooring lines

buoy

floating hose strings

anchor leg chain

buoyancy tanks

submarine pipeline

fluid swivel assembly

semi-gravity base

The LOOP system

is free to rotate in a 360-degree arc. It swings like a weathervane, always facing into the wind and waves.

Two parallel, flexible, floating hoses, each approximately 1,100 feet long, connect the ship's cargo manifold with the swivel unit in the base structure. The ship's pumps then begin to transfer the cargo ashore through an enormous submarine pipeline with a diameter of fifty-six inches.

The ship's pumps are not powerful enough to

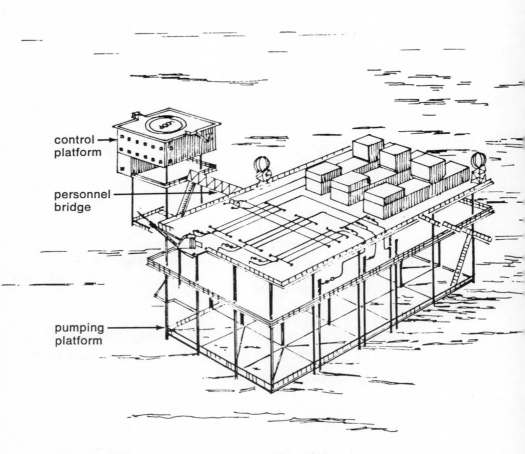

ship moored at buoy

control platform

personnel bridge

pumping platform

The LOOP pump platform boosts the oil flow from ship to shore.

118

push the crude all the way to shore, so a special pump platform rises out of the water about a mile and a half from the monobuoy. When the oil reaches the platform, it is boosted to shore by three 7,000-horsepower electric pumps. This pumping system is able to remove the oil from several tankers to shore-based underground storage facilities at rates of up to 100,000 barrels per hour.

Plans for LOOP call for three more mooring buoys. All six will spread out spokelike from a central pumping platform. When the billion-dollar complex is completed, it will be capable of handling nearly three and a half million barrels of crude oil a day. This amount is more than enough to supply the energy needs of the Midwest and parts of the South.

Still another way to get oil to places where big tankers cannot go is to transfer it at sea to several smaller vessels. To do so, a large tanker anchors in deep water offshore, and smaller ships nestle close to it. After they fill their tanks, they steam off for shallow-water ports. This process is called "transshipping," or "lightering." Because it can

Oil is lightered from a large to a canal-size vessel.

take five or six days, and a whole fleet of small vessels is needed, it is difficult and expensive.

However, lightering is essential for shipping oil through narrow canals and along shallow inland waterways. No canal in the world can accommodate a jumbo tanker. So without transshiping, oil could not go through the Suez Canal or the Panama Canal and would have to be carried all the way around Africa or South America.

To navigate the length of the Saint Lawrence Seaway, a vessel cannot have a draft of more than twenty-six feet or be over seventy-five feet wide. Tankers of this size usually fall in the 26,000-dwt class. For this reason, the small and aging World War II T-2 tankers are often seen among the bigger vessels plying the long seaway and crossing the Great Lakes.

Furthermore, the major rivers, including the Mississippi, the Missouri, the Ohio, and the Columbia, are all too shallow to take any seagoing tankers. So several transfers may take place before the oil is finally pumped aboard flat-bottomed barges that can safely navigate the inland waterways.

Perhaps the need to ship vast amounts of crude oil and petroleum products around the world will not always be as critical as it is now. Safe nuclear-based energy may eventually be developed to replace oil and natural gas; fuel-stingy machines may be built; solar power, hydropower, wind power, and even the energy of ocean tides may be harnessed to ease the critical need for fossil fuels. But these goals are considerably beyond the distant horizon. Until they are realized, the peoples of all developed nations will remain largely dependent on the energy locked into the molecules of oil and natural gas.

At present, the big ships—tankers—remain the primary available way to distribute these energy-producing fuels around the world.

Great flat-bottomed oil barges traverse shallow waterways.

GLOSSARY

Aft—toward the rear, or stern, of the ship.

Amidship—in or near middle of the ship.

Ballast—seawater or other heavy material carried low in the ship to increase stability.

Barrel—equals 42 United States gallons liquid measure.

Bilge—lowest part of the ship, near the keel.

Bitt—short deck post for securing ropes and cables.

Bow—front section of the ship.

Bridge—ship's control center, usually high atop the superstructure.

Bunker—tank in which fuel oil is carried.

Charter—to rent or lease rather than own a ship.

Chartroom—bridge area devoted largely to navigational planning.

Chock—deck-edged eye through which lines are fed ashore.

Crude oil—unrefined petroleum, as it comes from below ground.

Davit—a cranelike device for handling lifeboats, gangplanks, etc.

Deadweight ton (dwt)—carrying capacity of a ship measured in 2,240-pound long tons.

Deck—flat platform, or floor, of a ship.

Draft—depth of the keel below the waterline.

Fix—the ship's position as established by navigational procedures.

Forecastle (pronounced fōk´-s'l)—raised deck at ship's bow.

Freeboard—distance from main deck to waterline.

Galley—ship's kitchen.

Heading—direction in which ship is pointed.

Helmsman—crewman who steers the ship.

Hold—cargo storage area of the hull.

Hull—main body of the ship.

Keel—backbone of the ship, extending full length along its bottom.

Lighter—to transfer cargo from a large to a small ship.

Long ton—equals 2,240 pounds.

Main deck—the principal deck, stretching between a tanker's forecastle and superstructure.

Marisat—a sophisticated communication system, using relay satellites and shore stations

Master—captain, or skipper, of a ship.

Mate—deck officer below the captain.

Petrochemical—chemical product made from crude oil.

Petroleum—See crude oil.

Pitch—fore and aft vertical oscillation.

Plimsoll line—marks on the hull, indicating the legal loading limits of a ship.

Port—left side of ship.

Roll—a ship's side-to-side motion.

Rudder—vertical-hinged plate used to steer the ship through the water.

Seaman—crew member beneath the rank of officer.

Sextant—a navigational instrument that sights on celestial bodies to determine the ship's position.

Short ton—2,000 pounds.

Starboard—right side of ship.

Stern—rear or afterpart of ship.

Stores—food, water, laundry, and other ship's provisions.

Superstructure—where officers and seamen live and do most of their work.

Turbine—bladed wheel turned by boiler steam and geared to the propeller shaft.

Ultra Large Crude Carrier (ULCC)—a tanker that carries over 300,000 dwt's.

Very Large Crude Carrier (VLCC)—a tanker that carries between 160,000 and 300,000 dwt's.

Winch—a rotating drum for reeling in ropes or cables.

Windlass—a winchlike heavy-duty rotating cylinder used primarily to handle anchor chains.

INDEX

126

127

ABOUT THE AUTHOR

Charles (Chick) Coombs graduated from the University of California, at Los Angeles, and decided at once to make writing his career. While working at a variety of jobs, he labored at his typewriter early in the morning and late at night. An athlete at school and college, Mr. Coombs began by writing sports fiction. He soon broadened his interests, writing adventure and mystery stories, and factual articles as well. When he had sold over a hundred stories, he decided to try one year of full-time writing, chiefly for young people, and the results justified the decision.

Eventually he turned to writing books. To date he has published more than sixty books, both fiction and nonfiction, covering a wide range of subjects, from aviation and space, to oceanography, drag racing, motorcycling, and many others. He is also author of the Be a Winner series of books explaining how various sports are played and how to succeed in them.

Mr. Coombs and his wife, Eleanor, live in Westlake Village, near Los Angeles.